ROMANTIC
COUNTRY
– The Second Tale –

The Tale of the Secret Forest and the Animals of Cocot

A Fantasy Coloring Book

Eriy

St. Martin's Griffin

New York

Cocot, a land of beautiful forests, lakes,
and old townscapes where time seems to stand still,
has majestic castles lined up one after another.
The previous book in this series introduced us to the lives of the
genial folk of Cocot and their treatment of animals.

Romantic Country – The Second Tale – shows us an as yet
unexplored side of Cocot including the lives of fairies
that flutter about the country,
the witch who dwells at the heart of the forest, and much more.

Let's take a trip to some of the wonderful places in Cocot together
with Joset, the duck, and her friend, Elena.
You won't even need a passport or any large pieces of luggage!

Colored pencils, markers, ink, watercolors, etc...
All you need for this journey is your favorite painting material!
Paint with fantastic colors and create your own special
"ROMANTIC COUNTRY."

On another note, I would like to briefly explain the "lines"
that make up the images in this book.
All of the images were actually drawn with a toothpick.
I used approximately twelve hundred toothpicks to draw
everything in this book.
I hope you enjoy the truly simple and gentle lines,
unrenderable with a regular pen.

As your imagination expands, it will surely be fun to add lines and
write your own stories using toothpicks and ink.
You will be able to create your own original "special tale."
My greatest desire is for you to fully enjoy
Cocot in your own unique way.

Eriy

This is a map of Cocot with all the landmarks introduced in this book.

Krustallos Castle, Magleil Castle, the area where fairies live, the forest where the witch dwells, Sareine Alley, Polaris Clock Tower, etc. This map shows all of the places as they relate to the scenes introduced in this book.

Yowguste Forest

Krustallos Castle

Magleil Castle

Mahon's Flower

Crescent Lake

Mollis Sea

Polaris Clock Tower

CIRCUS

Taine River

POST OFFICE   CAFE   HENRY BOOKS

Sareine Alley

Ambrose Castle

Sareine Alley
and
Its Surroundings

The Fairies' Den

The Witch
Dwelling Forest

CHAPTER
1

The Glow of Beautiful Old Castles

CHAPTER
2

Magnificent Lakeside and Mountain Landscapes

BLUE BIRD'S LAUNDRY

SPECIMEN BOX
OF THE SEA

CHAPTER
3

Fairies and Works of Nature

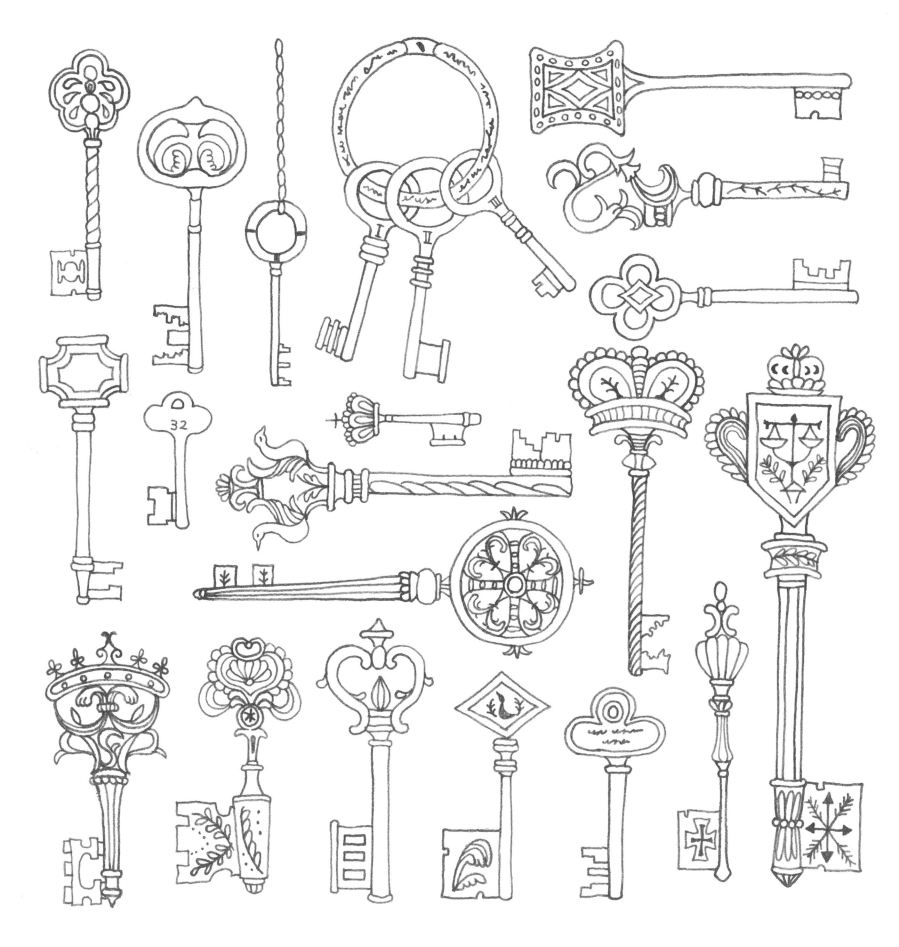

CHAPTER
4

The Witch and the Hidden
Secret Forest

CHAPTER
5

Cheerful Town Scenes

Chapter 1 allows you to see inside a few castles in Cocot and shows just how gorgeous the balls held at these castles can be.

A Garden in the Castle

This vegetable garden, where a whole variety of vegetables are grown, is surrounded by a castle wall. Children from town come to help during the harvest season.

Krustallos Castle

Since this castle is located in the northernmost reaches of Cocot, winter arrives there first. It seems as though snow has begun to fall already this year.

Christmas

As Christmas approaches, toy wooden soldiers are displayed in front of the gate. It has been said that originally they were displayed to protect everyone from misfortune.

A Castle's Food Pantry

Vegetables and fruits harvested in the garden are kept in this large food pantry. This is where the cooks from the castle come to decide on their daily menu.

Tea Time in June

On a beautiful day when hydrangeas are in full bloom, let's bring a table and chairs into the garden to enjoy some afternoon tea.

Coat of Arms

In Cocot, there are many castles and nobles' mansions. Each clan has its own coat of arms and practices various traditions that have been passed down through the generations.

The Night of a Full Moon

Since olden times it has been said that a full moon has some sort of "mysterious power." On such nights, you might be able to encounter fairies and witches rarely seen on ordinary nights.

Magleil Castle Coat of Arms

Designed with a unicorn and thistles, this is the coat of arms of Magleil Castle. At the foot of the unicorn there is an engraving in Latin with the words: "Moon," "Wonderful Land," and "Spring."

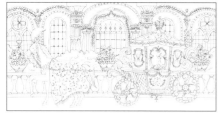

Going to the Ball

People in Cocot love going to the ball. When they receive an invitation, they dress up in their Sunday best and go to balls held at each castle.

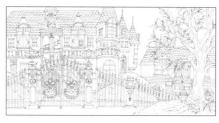

Count Spencer's Mansion

This is the mansion where Count Spencer and his wife live. They used to teach at a public school but now they teach social manners for children.

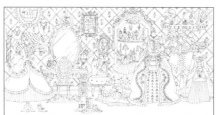

Madame Spencer's Closet

Madame Spencer prepares gowns and frocks for the children in town. Any one of the children can wear whichever outfit they choose.

A Night at the Ball

There are gorgeous gowns and fantastic music. Also, there is a veritable banquet of luxurious foods! Nights fly by during these dream-like balls.

In Chapter 2 we get a glimpse of Cocot's subjects' lives amongst all their magnificent nature. A beautiful flower garden and the calm lake heal each subject's heart.

The Sun and Moon Pipe Organ

There is a magnificent pipe organ at the church. It has been said that "playing the organ at night makes stars twinkle and playing it during the day makes the sun come out, thus causing crops to grow."

A Field of Flowers

There is a field near some windmills where carpets of flowers bloom. It is so nice to be able to just leisurely pick flowers.

Polaris Clock Tower

Beyond the lake you can see the Polaris Clock Tower. Seeing sunset from here calms you down and heals your heart.

Timothy, the Fawn

Timothy, the fawn, was just born this winter. He is very affectionate and rarely separated from his mother, whom he loves dearly.

Bird Houses

Hanging down from a large tree, each bird's house is very unique! There is a café, laundry, and delivery service too!

Ambrose III's Departure

Ambrose III, who created a map of Cocot, is departing on a new adventure with two egret brothers.

Mural on the Church Wall

The day before a wedding ceremony a new mural will be painted on the church's walls. This time, crocuses were drawn. The flower's meaning is "Believe In Me."

Uncle Willy's Barn

This barn belongs to Uncle Willy, the man who takes care of the flower fields. Flowers, planned for next year's planting, are already being grown in pots at the front door.

Church Stained Glass

This stained glass was created a long time ago. Despite the subtlety of the image, it shines magnificently when struck by the warm exterior light.

The Mysterious Cave

Once a decade, when the tide of Crescent Lake is low, this mysterious cave appears. Beautiful gems sleep untouched in this cave.

The Tree House

This used to be a "secret hideout" for Elena and Joset. It has now become a laboratory for plants that Elena found in Yowguste forest.

A Specimen Box of the Sea

Beautifully colored seashells and clypeasters. Rounded sea glass, a message bottle sent by someone ... these are all treasures discovered on the shores along the Morris sea.

Morris Sea

A beautiful coral reef spreads out through the clear, blue water of Morris Sea where sea creatures seem to live a life of leisure.

CHAPTER
3

Fairies and Works of Nature

All around Cocot charming fairies live in harmony with nature. Chapter 3 introduces us to the lives of these fairies.

Fairy Castle

The castle where the fairy queen lives is located where the most beautiful flowers bloom in spring. Each year, its location will vary, which is to say it is not easy to find this castle.

A Laboratory for Fairy Studies

Fairies are amazing creatures. This is Elena's office for fairy studies. A mountain of documents and collections are all lined up along the walls.

Leprechaun

This leprechaun is a shoemaker. No matter how worn-out a shoe is, he will repair it as good as new in no time. However, he only repairs one shoe?!

The Key to the Fairy's Den

There are several ways to get to the fairy's den, but the easiest is to find a "secret key." It is very tiny so be careful not to overlook it.

Leprechaun Trio

These leprechauns are mischievous. Today, it appears as though they have snuck in to tea-time in order to make their favorite "Candied Violet Petals."

Hawthorn Treehouse

This treehouse is home to three leprechauns. The fragrant Hawthorn tree is their favorite place to live! They are very friendly and will treat you to handmade hawthorn pies.

Mushroom Houses

Fairies love colorful mushrooms! As soon as they find their favorite mushroom, they will move into it at once.

Fairy Queen

Announcing the coming of spring is the duty of the fairy queen. When winter ends, the queen flies all over the country and makes sure that plants and flowers are ready to bloom.

Mermaid Castle

Deep down in the Morris Sea there is a place where mermaids live. Their castle made of seashells and beautiful coral is their greatest source of pride.

The Witch and the Hidden Secret Forest

Chapter 4 invites you to encounter witches that live in the heart of the thick forest. Please thoroughly enjoy this magical world filled with its mysterious charm.

Tea-Time with a Witch

Elena and Joset were invited to the witch's cottage for tea-time. However, this particular tea-time was like a dream. What with its tea that changed flavor every time you sipped it and its cookies that never seemed to end.

Love Potion

All you need to make a love potion is: a four-leafed clover, lilies of the valley, roses that bloomed on a snowy day, and a unicorn's tear drops.

Stores in an Alley

When you look up you see various-shaped playing cards. Below them, fabulous crafts are lined up. Go ahead and find your favorite.

A Witch's Castle

In a castle deep in the heart of the forest lives a beautiful witch. For centuries she has been maintaining her beauty, so nobody knows her real age.

Halloween Night

It has been said that "one can encounter a witch" if you dress up for Halloween and enter the forest at night. Alex and Mathew were both able to find the witch's house.

Witch Dwelling Forest

Deep in the heart of Yowguste forest, behind those ivied trees, Elena and Joset found a door that leads them into a world where witches dwell.

Magic Potion

You can get any type of medicine here, from terrifying potions to simple remedies for the common colds. For your sake, you'd best not ask about the ingredients.

Magician's Town

Everything a magician could possibly need is sold here, from the caldrons that are necessary to make magic potions, to flying blooms, and even pumpkins that transform into horses!?

Easter Witch

Hiding Easter eggs all over the country is her favorite act. Watching children joyfully searching for Easter eggs is her one true pleasure.

Mysterious Plants

The plants in this magic country are all quite mysterious - ivy continuously wraps around trees, shy flowers hide when you try to look at them, etc.

Magicians' Partner

Birds make very good partners for magicians. In the past crows were the popular choice, but now owls have taken over in popularity.

Chapter 5 is chock full of seasonal events held in Cocot. Can you hear the joyful laughter of the people thoroughly enjoying those events?

Preparations for Spring Festival

Before spring festival, Manon, the florist, displayed beautiful flowers all around the country. Peltier, her sister, and Joset came to help.

Henry Book

In Cocot, there is a tradition of giving a book to someone who is dear to you. At this book store, they have stacks of books brought in from all around the world. So, you can find the perfect gift anytime.

Madam Molly's Shop

Need a traditional costume worn on special days? Leave it to Madam Molly's shop! She does splendid work on the embroidery patterns passed down through each house.

Sewing Box

An antique thimble, berry pins that are passed down from grandma – Madam Molly's sewing box is full of treasures.

Marché

On holidays, the marché in Sareine Alley is open. You can buy various products like fresh fruits and homemade pies.

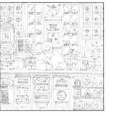

Post Master, Mr. Marcus

Mr. Marcus designs fabulous stamps and this is his post office. There are different mail boxes based on the type of letter being sent. Be careful not to make a mistake!

Stationery Sets

Mr. Marcus designs stationery sets exclusive to each castle. Magleil Castle's stationery is shown on this page.

Pancake Party

Pancake parties are held in the square near Sareine Alley! Pick any toppings you like and don't be shy, you can have as many pancakes as you like.

Circus Troupe

People have long awaited the arrival of a circus troupe, and this year one has finally arrived! Everyone is excited to hear the fun music and see the exceptional performances.

Puppet Show

The most popular play at the puppet show theater is the love story between Charlotte, the little ballerina, and Philip.

Yearly Cleaning

On New Year's Eve people gather to clean the Polaris Clock Tower. They carefully polish it and prepare to count out the days of the coming year.

Views from the Sky

Riding in a hot-air balloon and leisurely looking out over the town really feels fantastic. An unhurried journey through the sky can heals anyone's heart.

How to Enjoy the Attached Posters

You can enjoy the posters attached at the end of this book in many different ways. Paint the images with various colors, cut and paste them together, display them – enjoy them however you wish!

HOW TO PLAY 1
Color, Cut out, and then Assemble them for Displaying

Color the poster with various colors and cut out each image. After that let's play with them by pasting them on a base.
If you make copies of these images, you can enjoy them over and over by changing arrangements and combinations while imagining different situations.

1. Background
Fold along the margin found along the bottom for gluing. Fold slightly inward and then glue to the base.

2. The Base
This is the base that forms the background for individual images.

3. Individual Images
CASTLE: KNIGHT, BEAUTIFUL FLOWER, CHAIR, LUXURIOUS CANDLESTAND,
ELENA, JOSET, COUCH, FEAST
FOREST: TEA SET, KRUSTALLOS CASTLE, ABBEY, WITCH, JACK-O-LANTERN,
BROOM, WITCH HOUSE, BABY DEER TIMOTHY, JOSET, BASKET

Glue them onto the base by deciding each image's position.

HOW TO PLAY 2
Color and then Display on a Wall

Why don't you display your colored poster? There are many styles you can use. There is a simple one colored by a child, one that has an artistic finish using watercolor pencils, or one that has been dyed in black tea or oolong tea to make it appear antique. Please feel free to enjoy your own fantastic poster.

PATTERN A
-CASTLE-

PATTERN B
-FOREST-

1.

2.

3.

Eriy

Eriy is a toothpick illustrator. She worked as a designer for specialty items and apparel after graduating from Musashino Art University, and then became a freelance toothpick illustrator. Eriy is known for illustrations drawn with a toothpick and her travel diary illustrated with fantasy images using ballpoint pens and watercolor pencils. She has been broadening her field of activities not only in Japan but also overseas. Books, magazines, advertisements, websites, poster/packaging illustrations, etc. Eriy has drawn illustrations for many different types of media. She is also active as a designer. She is the author of *Romantic Country* (St. Martin's Griffin).

Homepage	http://cocot-eriy.jimdo.com
Blog	http://yaplog.jp/eriy_cafe
Instagram	Eriy06

ROMANTIC COUNTRY THE SECOND TALE: A COLORING BOOK by Eriy
Text, images and design copyright © 2015 Eriy and Graphic-sha Publishing Co., Ltd.

First designed and published in Japan in 2015 by Graphic-sha Publishing Co., Ltd.

English edition published in the United States of America in 2016 by St. Martin's Press
175 Fifth Avenue, New York, N.Y. 10010, the USA

www.stmartins.com

ISBN 978-1-250-11728-1

Our books may be purchased in bulk for promotional, educational, or business use.
Please contact your local bookseller or the Macmillan Corporate and Premium Sales Departmentat
at 1-800-221-7945, extension 5442, or by e-mail at MacmillanSpecialMarkets@macmillan.com.

First U.S. Edition: December 2016

Printed and bound in China

10 9 8 7 6 5 4 3 2

Creative staff

Author:	Eriy
Planning and editing:	Harumi Shinoya
Illustrations:	Eriy
Book design:	Mari Kunou

English edition

| English translation: | Kevin Wilson |
| English edition layout: | Shinichi Ishioka |

This edition was coordinated by LibriSource Inc.

Production and management: Graphic-sha Publishing Co., Ltd.